C903228295

D0318430

Science Technology Engineering Maths

STEM STARTERS FOR KIDS

THE ESSENTIAL GUIDE TO S.T.E.A.M.

LIBRARIES NI
WITHDRAWN FROM STOCK

Written by Eryl Nash

with contributions by Jenny Jacoby,
Sam Hutchinson & Catherine Bruzzone

Designed and illustrated by

Vicky Barker

www.bsmall.co.uk

British Library Cataloguing-in-Publication Data.

A catalogue record for this book is available from the British Library.

Published by
b small publishing ltd.

www.bsmall.co.uk

· 1 2 3 4 5 ·

Design and art direction by Vicky Barker
Additional design by Christian Francis
Production by Madeleine Ehm
Printed in China by WKT Co. Ltd.

text and illustrations copyright © b small publishing 2019

All rights reserved. No reproduction, copy or transmission of this publication may be made without written permission. No part of this publication may be reproduced, stored in a retrieval system, or transmitted in any form or by any means, electronic, mechanical, photocopying, recording or otherwise without the prior permission of the publisher.

ISBN
978-1-911509-93-6

WHAT IS STEAM?

STEAM stands for 'science, technology, engineering, art and mathematics'. These areas are closely linked: engineers couldn't do their jobs without science, technology or maths. Art techniques and ways of thinking can inspire science, technology, engineering and maths, just as they can inspire art. Together, STEAM can help solve problems and make our lives better in ways that hadn't been possible before.

Science   Technology   Engineering   Art   Maths

OBSERVING ODDITIES

The materials that objects are made from have their own characteristics. These characteristics are a bit like their personality and help us to decide what to use them for. For example, some materials are very easy to squash or squish or twist, and other materials are very hard to squash or squish or twist. It is important to use a material with the correct characteristics to result in a product that works.

This hammer is made from **bendy** material.

Top scientists use big words to describe their observations properly. They will use words like **opaque** (you cannot see through it) or **transparent** (you can see through it) so we know exactly what they are looking at.

This liquid is colourful and **opaque**.

This wrapping paper is **transparent** so we can see inside.

This cushion is made from very **rough** material.

This scarf is very **stiff** and difficult to wear.

The characteristics of a material can change. Water becomes snow or ice under **0 degrees Celsius** and it becomes steam very quickly over **100 degrees Celsius**.

ELECTRICITY

Electricity is a power that comes from tiny particles called **electrons.** Electrons are in every material in the world – from your clothes to your food and your hair – but it is when they flow in one direction that they produce electricity.

Electrons have a small charge, and when lots of electrons group together that charge can get large enough to be powerful.

In nature you can see electricity when lightning shoots through the sky. Lightning is a huge number of electrons flowing through the air at once, trying to escape to the earth, releasing an explosion of light.

Has your hair ever stood on end when you've brushed it, or rubbed a balloon on it? That is electricity too! The hairbrush or balloon passes electrons to your hair, and when so many electrons group together they push each other apart, taking your hair with it.

When we cause the electrons to flow in wires (by using batteries or plugging them into the mains at the wall) the electricity can be useful. Their power can turn on things we attach to the wire circuits – from lightbulbs to dishwashers.

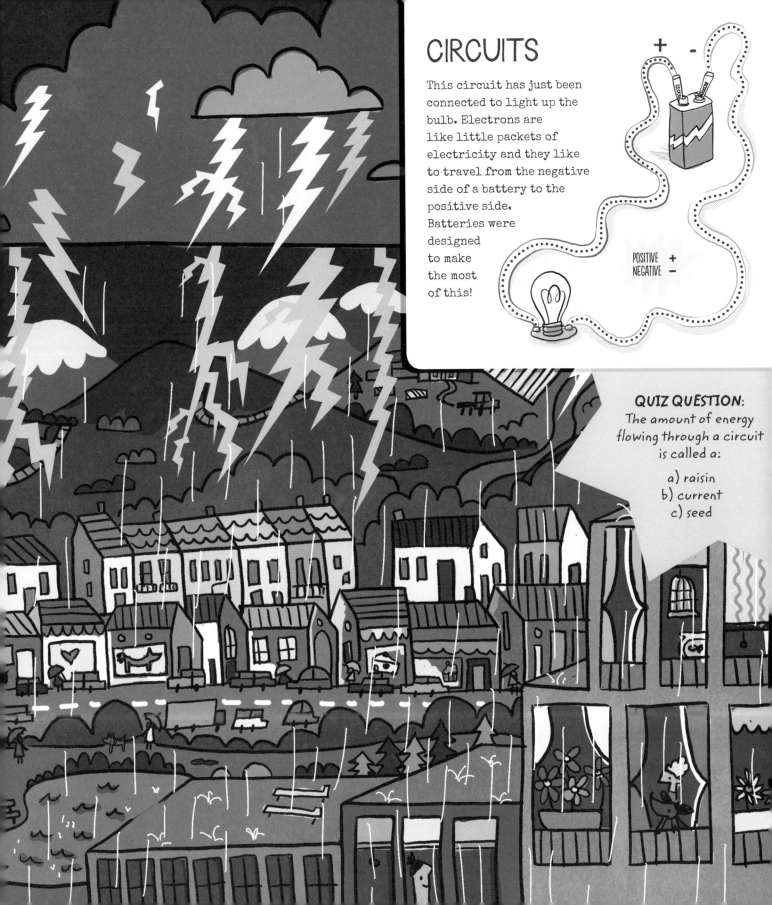

CIRCUITS

This circuit has just been connected to light up the bulb. Electrons are like little packets of electricity and they like to travel from the negative side of a battery to the positive side. Batteries were designed to make the most of this!

POSITIVE +
NEGATIVE —

+ -

QUIZ QUESTION:
The amount of energy flowing through a circuit is called a:

a) raisin
b) current
c) seed

TYPES OF ENERGY

The turbines in power plants spin to create electricity. Different methods are used to make the turbines turn, but the most popular way is to use steam. The electricity then travels along power cables to your home.

OLD ENERGY

Coal, gas and oil are made from plants and animals that died a long time ago and have been buried under soil and rocks ever since. Once these fuels have heated the water to make steam in power plants they cannot be used again. They create pollution that harms the environment.

NEW ENERGY

Wind turbines and hydro dams (hydro means 'water' in Ancient Greek) use wind or water, instead of steam, to make the turbines in a power station turn. Wind and water are called **green energy** because they can be used again and again. This is good for the environment.

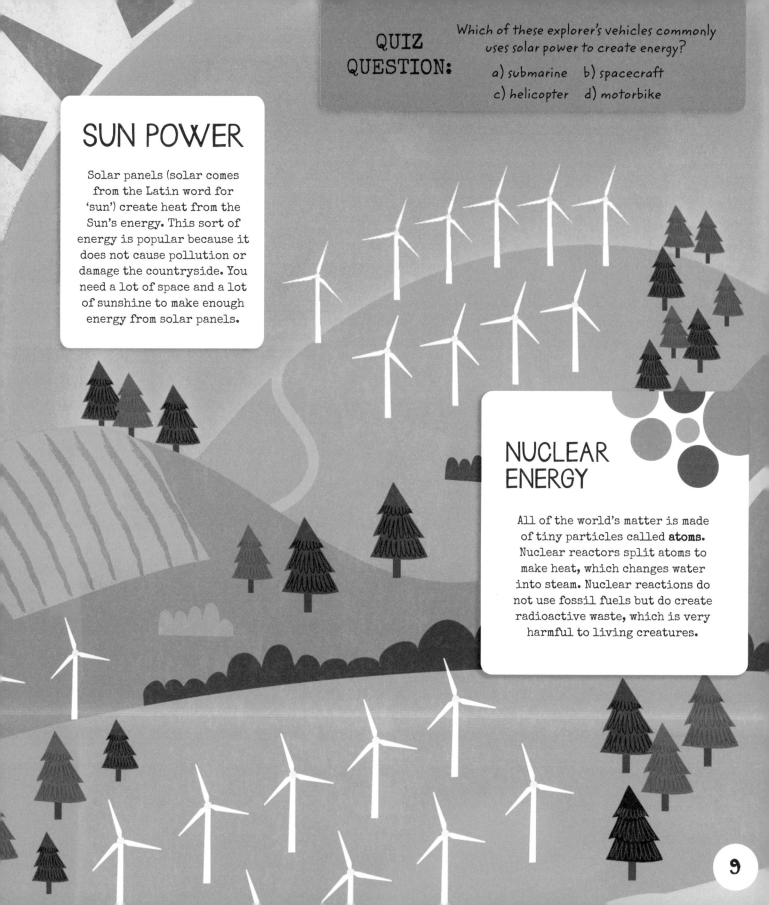

Which of these explorer's vehicles commonly uses solar power to create energy?

a) submarine   b) spacecraft
c) helicopter   d) motorbike

SUN POWER

Solar panels (solar comes from the Latin word for 'sun') create heat from the Sun's energy. This sort of energy is popular because it does not cause pollution or damage the countryside. You need a lot of space and a lot of sunshine to make enough energy from solar panels.

NUCLEAR ENERGY

All of the world's matter is made of tiny particles called **atoms**. Nuclear reactors split atoms to make heat, which changes water into steam. Nuclear reactions do not use fossil fuels but do create radioactive waste, which is very harmful to living creatures.

SOUND

Sound travels in 'waves'. A thing making a sound vibrates. Those vibrations make sound waves, which travel in all directions through gases (the air), liquids and solids. To hear a sound, you need an ear, which can turn sound waves into messages that are sent to your brain about what you're hearing.

The guitar string vibrates.

Sound waves travel through the air.

An ear picks up the sound wave.

Sound waves travel at different speeds depending on what they're travelling through. On a warm day, sound travels through air at 344 metres per second. On a hot day, sound travels faster. But sound travels faster still through liquids, like water, and some solids, like rock and metal. Other materials, like foam, are bad at transmitting sound waves and people use them to 'sound proof' or catch sound waves and stop them from travelling on.

TYPES OF SOUND

The type of sound that you hear depends on the **wavelength** (distance between the same point on two waves), **amplitude** (height of the sound wave) and **frequency** (number of waves per second).

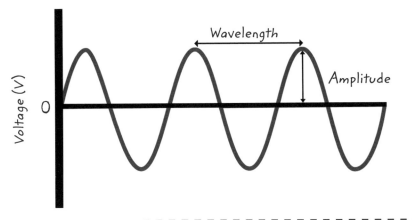

LION'S ROAR
This sound has a higher **AMPLITUDE** than the mouse's, so the sound is louder.

MOUSE'S SQUEAK
This sound has a higher **FREQUENCY** than the lion's, so it has a higher pitch.

DID YOU KNOW?

There is no sound in space! But here on Earth, the loudest natural sound is of an erupting volcano.

LIGHT

Light travels much, much faster than sound. In just one second, light can travel all the way to the Moon. In that time, sound has only travelled the length of three football pitches. That's why, in a storm, you often see lightning a few seconds before you hear the thunder, even though the two start at exactly the same moment.

Light cannot travel around a corner. Light bounces off objects and we see objects because of the light that bounces off them. That is why we can't see things in the dark, and why we can't see things around corners.

One way to see around a corner is to use a mirror. Because the mirror is a shiny, reflective surface, the light bounces off it in another direction.

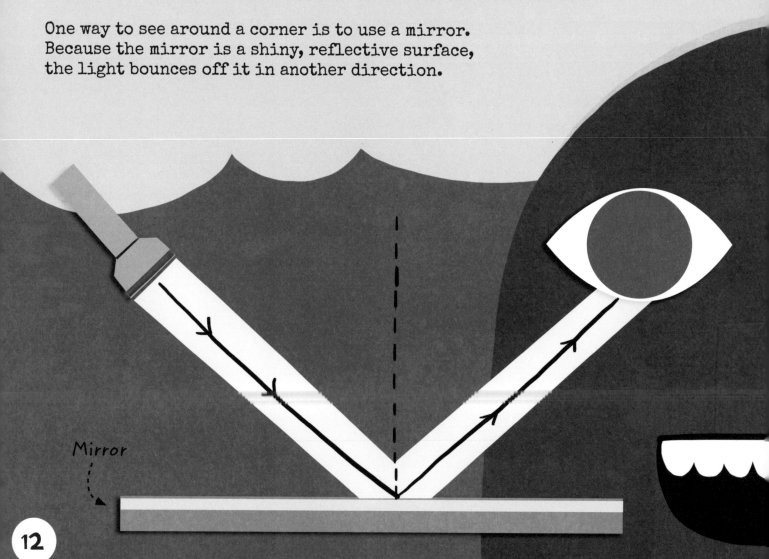

Mirror

SHADOW MAGIC

When there is something between an object and light, that thing casts a shadow. The Sun is our main source of natural light. During the day, light reflects off objects and into our eyes so that we can see them. Shadows are examples of darkness that we can see.

Indoors, when it's dark, you can use a torch to create shadows with your hands.

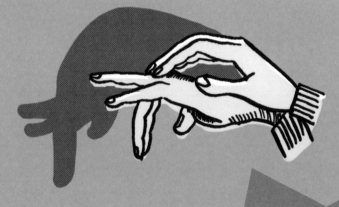

QUIZ QUESTION:

Our main natural source of light is:

a) the Sun
b) the Moon
c) a light switch

MAGNETS

A magnet is a piece of rock or metal that can pull certain other metals towards it. Like electricity, magnetism is a natural force that humans have learned to make use of. Material becomes **magnetised** when all of its electrons spin in the same direction and create a magnetic field.

Magnets attract metals that have iron in them, like steel and nickel. Materials such as wool, glass, wood or plastic are not magnetic.

Magnetic field —
the area affected by the magnet

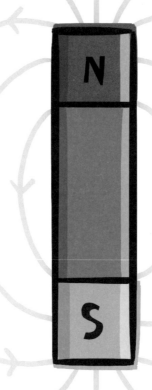

N

S

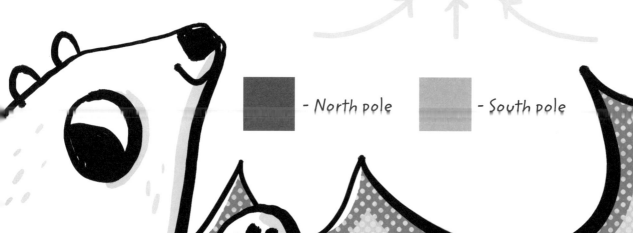

- North pole   - South pole

OPPOSITES ATTRACT

A magnet has two opposite ends: a north pole and a south pole. Opposites attract, so the north pole of a magnet will **ATTRACT** south poles from other magnets but it will **PUSH AWAY** north poles. The south pole attracts north poles and repels south poles.

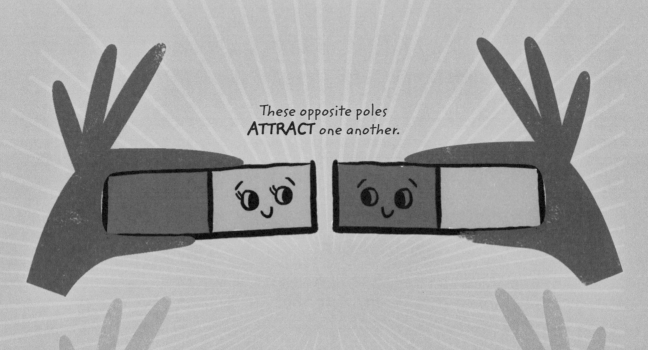

These opposite poles **ATTRACT** one another.

These identical poles **REPEL** one another.

DID YOU KNOW?

There is a magnetic field all around us because the Earth is like a giant magnet. That's why a compass will always point towards the North Pole.

QUIZ QUESTION:

Magnetism is a type of what?
a) electricity
b) gravity
c) force

GRAVITY

Gravity is an invisible force that pulls things towards the ground. It is why when we jump in the air, we always land back down and don't keep on flying up into the sky.

Each planet has its own force of gravity, and it is different on different planets. The bigger the planet, the bigger the gravity. On planets smaller than Earth, gravity is less strong. So you would feel a lot lighter and be able to jump higher than you can on Earth.

Although gravity has been around since the universe began, it was only discovered about 300 years ago, when Sir Isaac Newton noticed an apple falling out of a tree and realised there was a force making that happen.

Sun

16

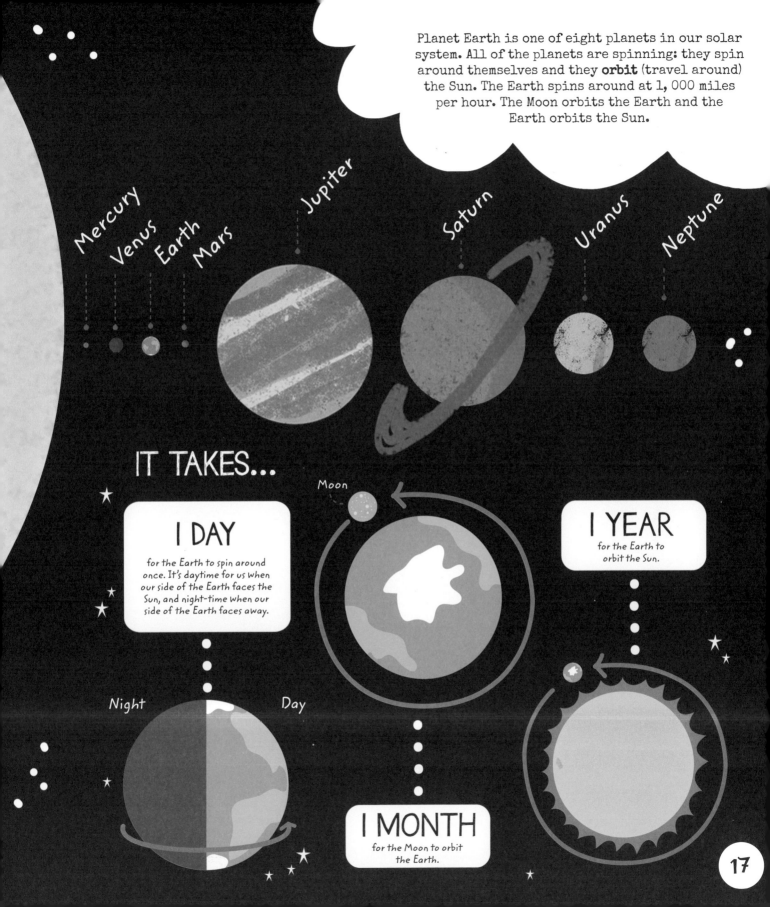

Planet Earth is one of eight planets in our solar system. All of the planets are spinning: they spin around themselves and they **orbit** (travel around) the Sun. The Earth spins around at 1, 000 miles per hour. The Moon orbits the Earth and the Earth orbits the Sun.

Mercury
Venus
Earth
Mars
Jupiter
Saturn
Uranus
Neptune

IT TAKES...

I DAY

for the Earth to spin around once. It's daytime for us when our side of the Earth faces the Sun, and night-time when our side of the Earth faces away.

Moon

I YEAR

for the Earth to orbit the Sun.

Night   Day

I MONTH

for the Moon to orbit the Earth.

THE BIG BANG

Physicists believe that the universe was created about 14 billion years ago, when the 'big bang' happened. It was a giant explosion that turned energy into matter, and over a very long time that matter developed into our universe, including our galaxy, our solar system and Earth as we know it.

One reason people believe in the big bang theory is because physics tells us how much of certain chemical elements exist in the universe, and that quantity matches what we think was created in the big bang.

The **UNIVERSE** is made up of more stars than we can count, in billions of galaxies.

A **GALAXY** is a collection of millions or billions of stars, held together by gravity.

MATTER is a word physicists use for anything that takes up space – from atoms to rocks and people.

FORCES

Understanding how objects move starts with understanding forces. Forces are pushes and pulls. All around us, forces are acting on everything.

If the same amount of force pushes an object in one direction as there is pushing it in the opposite direction, the object won't change its motion. So if it was sitting still, it will remain still, or if it was moving, it will keep moving in the same way. These are 'balanced' forces.

If the amount of force pushing an object in one direction is bigger or smaller than a force pushing it in the opposite direction, the object will change its motion. So if it was sitting still, it may start moving, or if it was moving, it may change direction or begin to move more quickly or slowly. These are 'unbalanced' forces.

SPEEDING UP, SLOWING DOWN

An object will only move if a big enough force – like a push, pull or gravity – acts on it. When you kick a ball, your kick is the force, so the ball then **accelerates** (a big word for 'speeds up') across the ground. The ball goes from standing still to moving fast.

DID YOU KNOW?

Sir Isaac Newton was the scientist who developed theories about forces. He came up with three 'laws of motion' which explain why objects do or don't move.

There are two things to know about how objects behave when they accelerate:

1: The heavier an object is, the less easy it is to accelerate (a light ball will start moving more easily than a heavy ball).

2: The bigger the force acting on the object (the kick to the ball), the more it will accelerate (the faster the ball will go).

EQUAL & OPPOSITE

Forces always act in pairs. When an object pushes against another object, the second object pushes back just as hard in the opposite direction – even if it is not possible to see or feel. This is because for every action, there is an EQUAL and OPPOSITE reaction.

If forces are always equal and opposite, how does a force ever make anything move? When we say that forces are 'equal and opposite', that doesn't mean they cancel each other out. There are always other forces involved, too.

When you push a toy truck with your finger, the truck pushes back against your finger with just as much force - equal and opposite. But you don't move because of other forces acting on your body. The truck does move because the force you apply is enough to overcome all the other forces acting on the truck.

So, although the forces are equal and opposite, the forces between different objects do not have exactly the same effect on one another.

FRICTION

Friction is a force between two objects that are touching. When two objects move against each other, friction can make heat and sound, and slow down movement. Some objects cause more friction than others. The rougher an object is, the more friction it makes – so objects designed to grip and stay put are made of rough material and built in bulky shapes. The smoother an object is, the less friction it produces – so objects designed to travel quickly are made of smooth material and built in smooth shapes.

EVERLASTING ENERGY

Energy is the ability to do work. You use energy to walk up the stairs just as a ball uses energy to roll down a slope. The amazing thing about energy is that it never runs out! It never runs out but it does change form. When it looks like the energy has gone away – when the ball reaches the bottom of the slope and stops – it hasn't disappeared, just changed.

The ball is full of **gravitational potential energy**, which means it has the potential to move downwards with the pull of gravity.

Some of the ball's gravitational potential energy has changed to **sound energy** and some has changed to **movement (or 'kinetic') energy**. Some gravitational potential energy still remains due its potential to keep rolling down the slope.

The ball is still again, and all of its sound and movement energy has now changed into other forms of energy, such as **heat (or 'thermal') energy**.

MEASUREMENTS

Measurements are important for scientists and engineers to be able to carry out experiments and come up with theories. But they are also important for everyday life – such as for knowing how much medicine to take, or how much of each ingredient to use in cooking. **Weight, volume** and **length** are all categories of measurements.

Mathematicians use symbols to help them perform calculations more quickly on paper.

This sign means 'equal to' and is used when measuring accurately.

≈

This sign means 'approximately equal to' and is used when estimating measurements.

SOME USEFUL EVERYDAY MEASUREMENTS

1 cm ≈ the width of a pencil

3 cm ≈ the length of a cherry tomato

50 cm ≈ the height of a sheet of A4 paper

1 m ≈ the width of a single bed

2 m ≈ the height of a door in a house

LENGTH

There are lots of ways to measure lengths. You can use a ruler or tape measure to measure accurately, or you can **estimate** – which is a bit like clever guessing. Estimating takes practice but there are some tricks to help you. When you know the average size of an everyday object – like the length of a pencil – you can use this information to estimate the measurements of other things around you.

VOLUME

Capacity – also called **volume** – is a measure of how much space something takes up. You can measure the capacity of things that can be poured from one container to another. Capacity can be measured in millilitres (ml) and litres (l), and there are 1,000 millilitres in a litre. However, you might see capacity measured in all sorts of ways...

a pinch   a drop   a teaspoon   a tablespoon   a cup

QUIZ QUESTION:

How many metres are there in a kilometre?

a) 10

b) 100

c) 1,000

WEIGHT

Bigger things aren't necessarily heavier than smaller things. A pillow filled with feathers is larger than a brick, but the brick is heavier. We can measure weight by using scales. The metric scale measures in grams (g) and kilograms (kg). There are 1,000 grams in a kilogram.

CALCULATIONS

Calculations help us work out what happens when we add to something, take away something, or divide something up.

Here's an example. This cake has 8 slices. If it is shared equally between 4 guests, each guest will get 2 slices. That means that 8 divided by 4 equals 2.

SHARING

Sharing things out is called **division.** Things can be shared out evenly but sometimes there will be leftovers known as the **remainder.**

This loaf of bread has 13 slices. If it is shared equally between 5 guests, each guest will get 2 slices – but there will be 3 slices remaining. That means that 13 divided by 5 equals 2, but with a remainder of 3.

This is the remainder.

MULTIPLES

Multiplication is adding the same number to itself an amount of times. So 3 x 3 means to add 3 to itself three times, or 3 + 3 + 3. Both methods give the answer.

You can represent 3 x 3 in a grid, too, where there are 3 rows and 3 columns, like this:

Or you can show 2 x 4, like this:

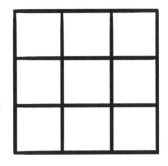
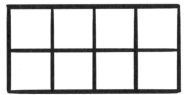

ROUNDING UP

Sometimes it's easier to understand larger numbers if they are rounded up or down to something simpler.

Numbers ending 1 to 4 are rounded down to the nearest 0. So 13 becomes 10. Numbers ending 5 to 9 are rounded up to the nearest 0. So 27 becomes 30.

You can also round off numbers and use other words to describe numbers.

roughly

more than

almost

less than

about

TAKEAWAYS

Things are taken away – or **subtracted** – in all sorts of everyday situations. Some things are simple to count, if they are all the same size and shape, such as squares of a chocolate bar. Other things, like liquids, have to be measured in fractions (or equal parts) of a whole unit. The whole unit could be an official way of measuring, such as litres, or anything useful, like a bottle or cup.

This bottle was full to the top. One quarter (1/4) of the bottle has been used, so three quarters (3/4) are left.

This bar had 30 squares of chocolate. 7 squares of chocolate have been eaten, so there are 23 squares left.

CREATIVE THINKING

Scientists and engineers always need to be creative – they need to think up new questions to answer, and clever ways to solve problems. Here are some of the ways that art can help scientists and engineers with new ideas and information.

DRAWING DATA

When scientists do research they come up with **data** – the numbers and results of their research. Often this data will be in a table or a list. While that information can be very useful, it is not always going to look very interesting. A table of data is the purest way of presenting information, but information could be presented in as many ways as you can imagine.

SKETCHING

An art skill that can really help to communicate your ideas is sketching. This can be useful for anybody working in a team who has an idea the whole group should understand, and sometimes drawing the idea can be the quickest way to express it.

I. A description

"Last night Daddy cooked spaghetti bolognese for us all to eat, but Mummy said she only wanted some soup, and my brother wanted his favourite food instead, so in the end only Dad and I ate pasta, and my brother had fish fingers."

2. A table

PERSON	FOOD
Mum	Soup and bread
Dad	Spaghetti bolognese
Phoebe	Spaghetti bolognese
Harry	Fish fingers, chips and peas

3. A picture

Mum

Dad

Phoebe

Harry

MIND MAPS

A mind map is a drawing of an idea. It is a way to draw all your thoughts about an idea in one place so you can see links you hadn't thought about. This could be useful for a team of scientists or engineers trying to solve a problem or come up with new ideas. Why just have a list when you could have a beautiful mind map that you might even want to hang on your wall and look at? Here's how.

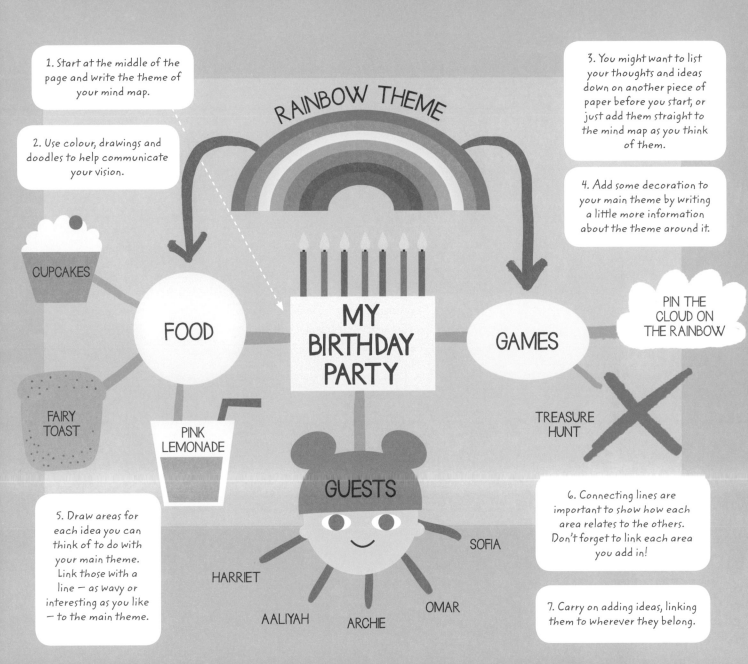

1. Start at the middle of the page and write the theme of your mind map.

2. Use colour, drawings and doodles to help communicate your vision.

3. You might want to list your thoughts and ideas down on another piece of paper before you start, or just add them straight to the mind map as you think of them.

4. Add some decoration to your main theme by writing a little more information about the theme around it.

5. Draw areas for each idea you can think of to do with your main theme. Link those with a line — as wavy or interesting as you like — to the main theme.

6. Connecting lines are important to show how each area relates to the others. Don't forget to link each area you add in!

7. Carry on adding ideas, linking them to wherever they belong.

RAINBOW THEME

CUPCAKES

FOOD

FAIRY TOAST

PINK LEMONADE

MY BIRTHDAY PARTY

GUESTS

HARRIET

AALIYAH

ARCHIE

OMAR

SOFIA

GAMES

PIN THE CLOUD ON THE RAINBOW

TREASURE HUNT

SHAPES ALL AROUND US

Words like **geometry** and **symmetry** are used by mathematicians. They describe things that are part of our everyday lives – you just need to look out for them!

SPIRALS

There are so many examples of spirals in nature. Once you know to look for them you can find them in all sorts of places.

SYMMETRY

Many things in nature are symmetrical. That means that two halves are exactly the same. Butterflies are symmetrical because each half has exactly the same pattern. Snowflakes are even more specially symmetrical because it doesn't matter where you divide them in two, each half will always be symmetrical.

RIGHT ANGLES

When two straight lines meet they make an angle. A **right angle** is a special kind of angle, shaped like an 'L' – once you can recognise a right angle you'll see they are all around us.

GEOMETRY

Geometry is a part of mathematics that is all about shapes. So many beautiful patterns can be made with shapes. Using some simple art skills – like colouring and drawing lines – can make them more beautiful and also help to show off the shapes inside the patterns even more clearly.

GROUNDBREAKING TECHNOLOGY

Technology is the practical application of scientific knowledge by engineers and scientists. Their aim is to improve the things around us. Not all technology is shiny and digital. The best inventions are those that everybody can benefit from.

Johannes Gutenberg

PRINTING PRESS

Back in the Middle Ages, books were hand-written and then copied out (mostly by teams of monks). This meant there were very few copies of books, and each one was very expensive. The engineer who solved the problem of books being such hard work to make was Johannes Gutenberg. His solution was mechanical printing with 'moveable type' – lots of copies of each letter of the alphabet, made out of metal. Printers could combine these in different ways in a printing press to make any number of copies of any text.

DID YOU KNOW?

Moveable type was actually used in Asia for hundreds of years before Gutenberg's invention. But Gutenberg developed a press that could mechanically transfer ink from the moveable type to paper. This was the first printing press.

123

Moveable type goes into a printing press back-to-front. This is so it appears the right way round when printed on paper.

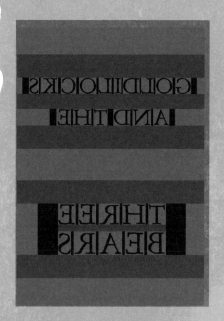

GOLDILOCKS AND THE

THREE BEARS

THE TELEGRAPH

The printing press helped knowledge to spread more quickly. But another engineering invention which helped people communicate ideas and information was the telegraph. Developed by Samuel Morse and other inventors, it allowed electrical signals to be sent along a wire. Morse also developed what we now call the Morse Code – a way to transmit messages along the wires. All of this led the way to today's telephone.

TALKING ON THE TELEPHONE

Before telephones were invented, if you wanted to talk to someone, you had to go to their house or meet them somewhere face to face. Now you can talk to friends on the other side of the world just by picking up the phone.

G'DAY!

¡HOLA!

HI!

NAMASTE!

MOBILE PHONES

When you speak into a mobile phone, it sends a microwave to a special mast and this mast transmits (sends) it on to the telephone exchange. The exchange turns it into a digital message to send on to the person you are speaking to, along a cable or sometimes by satellite.

SNAP HAPPY

Before the invention of digital cameras, if you wanted a portrait of yourself or your favourite pet, an artist had to paint it for you. Early cameras were very large and heavy and took ages to take the photo. Now digital cameras are small and light and you can take photos with a tiny camera in a mobile phone.

QUIZ QUESTION:

When were mobile phones first invented?

a) less than 50 years ago
b) around 100 years ago
c) more than 100 years ago

Images taken by your camera that look smooth are actually made of lots of squares.

When you point your camera at something, light travels from the scene or object you are photographing into the camera through a lens. This light then hits a sensor, which is divided into millions of little squares, called **pixels**.

Each pixel represents a different colour or brightness. The computer in the camera converts the pixels into a picture.

LEVERS, HINGES AND CATAPULTS

CATAPULTS

Medieval castles and cities were defended by big, strong walls. Before the invention of gunpowder, catapults were the best weapon to attack a city or castle. The arm holding the stones is held down, under tension, so it is trying to pull away from whatever is holding it down. When the tension is released, the arm swings round and shoots out the stone. Catapults could shoot heavy stones and even rotting animal bodies!

LEVER

FULCRUM

LEVERS

Catapults are based on levers. Levers are one of the oldest machines in the world, and they help to lift things that would be too heavy to lift by yourself. Levers need something called a **fulcrum** to balance on. By changing the position of the heavy and light things along the lever, heavy things can be lifted more easily. Something light can help lift something heavy if the heavy thing is close to the fulcrum and the light thing is far from it.

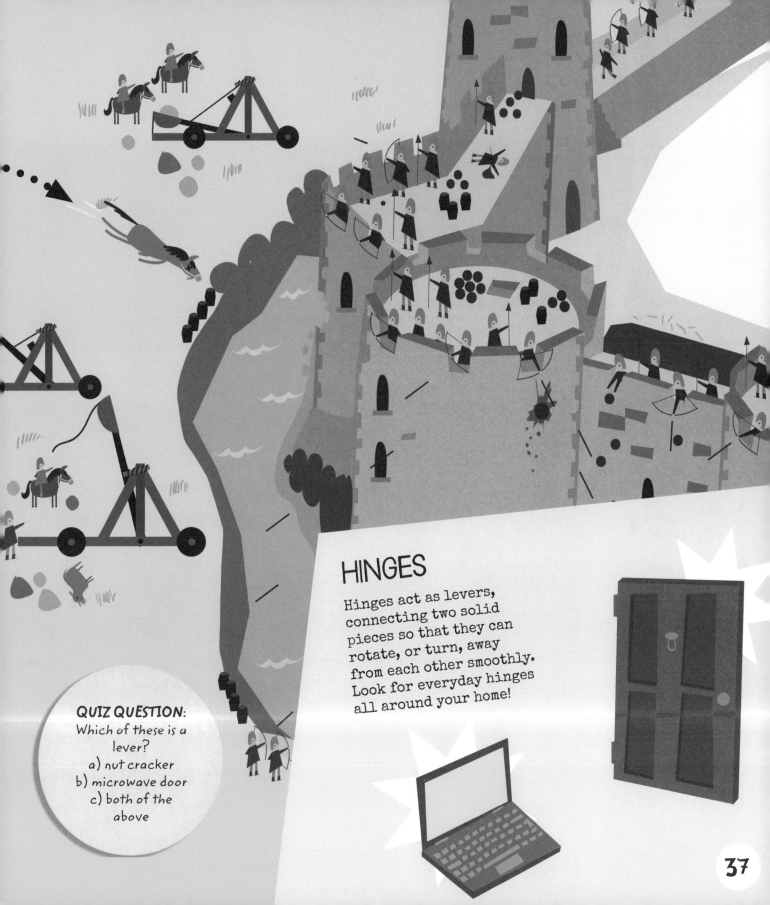

HINGES

Hinges act as levers, connecting two solid pieces so that they can rotate, or turn, away from each other smoothly. Look for everyday hinges all around your home!

QUIZ QUESTION:
Which of these is a lever?
a) nut cracker
b) microwave door
c) both of the above

UP IN THE SKY

FLYING PLANES

The problem of how to get a large metal aeroplane, filled with people and luggage, to fly in the sky seems impossible to solve. But one thing that helped engineers to come up with a solution is the shape of the wings.

Aeroplane wings are shaped like an aerofoil. When the plane travels forward quickly (when it speeds up along a runway), the air finds it quicker and easier to move the shorter distance underneath the wing than to travel up over the bump of the wing. With more air underneath the wing, the wing lifts up, taking the aeroplane with it.

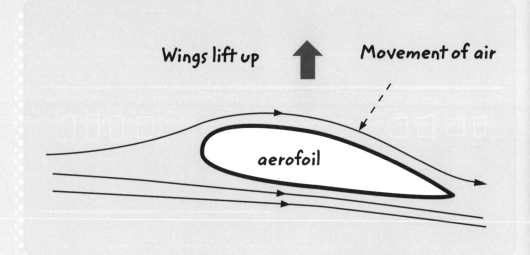

Wings lift up

Movement of air

aerofoil

DID YOU KNOW?
An engineer who designs planes is called an **aeronautical engineer.**

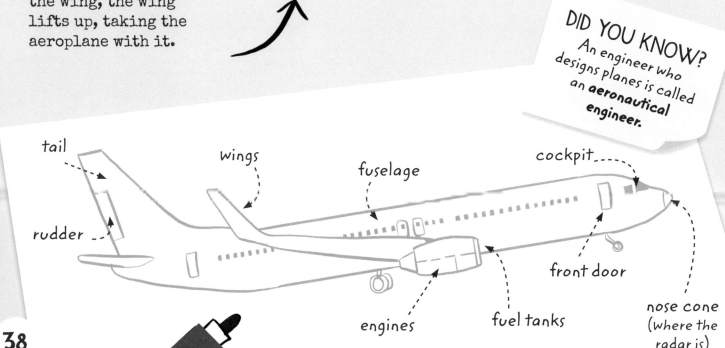

tail

wings

fuselage

cockpit

rudder

front door

engines

fuel tanks

nose cone
(where the radar is)

PARACHUTES

When a person jumps out of an aeroplane gravity pulls them down to earth but **air resistance** slows them down. A person without a parachute has very little resistance against the air and falls quickly. Because parachutes make a large canopy, they collect a lot of air. This increases the air resistance, so they fall more slowly.

EJECTOR SEATS

Air force pilots sometimes have to get out of their aircraft quickly to save their lives. They use an ejector seat. First, the pilot pulls a handle and the roof of the plane explodes off. A catapult then pushes the seat along some rails and out of the plane. Then a small rocket fires it away from the plane. Next, a small parachute opens to slow the seat down. Finally the small parachute pulls the main parachute out and the seat is shot away, so the pilot can float to earth safely!

DID YOU KNOW?

The highest ever freefall parachute jump was from 41,422 metres (135,898.68 feet) above the Earth, set by Alan Eustace in 2014.

SOLVING PROBLEMS

Engineers have to pay attention to all sorts of things going on in the world to notice problems they could help with. They need to be very creative to find ways of solving those problems.

ECO PACKAGING

A problem facing us all is what to do with packaging when we don't need it anymore. Engineers have come up with some clever ways to reduce the amount of packaging we throw away and the amount of rubbish that builds up on the planet. One way of doing this is by making packaging from reused materials. But the best type of packaging breaks down by itself when you throw it away – this is **biodegradable** material. Some packaging even has seeds built into it, so if the packaging is buried the seeds can grow in the ground.

EARTHQUAKE-PROOF

Engineers have thought of ways to stop buildings from falling down when there is an earthquake. People can survive being on quaking ground but they are in danger if a building falls on them. One way to 'earthquake-proof' a building is to let it wobble safely with the quake. The more it can wobble, the less likely it is to fall down and injure people.

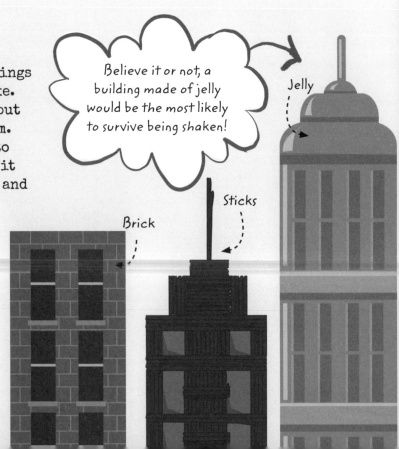

Believe it or not, a building made of jelly would be the most likely to survive being shaken!

Jelly

Sticks

Brick

QUIZ QUESTION:

Which country has the most recorded earthquakes in the world?

a) China
b) Fiji
c) Japan

RUNNING BLADES

Engineers have helped people without lower legs solve the problem of how to walk and run. Running blades are made from a very-strong-but-light material called 'carbon fibre' and the way they are shaped makes them bendy like a spring. This springiness helps the runner to sprint forwards in the same way as a natural leg does.

WHEELY USEFUL

A wheelchair means that people who have difficulty walking can go to work, visit friends, go shopping and play sports. Wheelchairs can be electric and are powered by batteries. Some wheelchairs have large rubber wheels so they can go on snow or into water. Sports wheelchairs need to be much lighter than standard wheelchairs so the athlete can whizz around the court.

ENGINEERING FUN

GLOW STICKS

Glow sticks are great fun for parties but they only glow for a few hours. There are three ingredients inside a glow stick and as soon as they mix together it starts to glow. How do engineers solve the problem of the glow sticks glowing before someone is ready to use them? They keep one of the ingredients separate from the others in a small glass tube.
When you want to make the stick glow, you snap the tube and shake – this mixes all three ingredients together!

1.   2.   SNAP!   3.

DID YOU KNOW?

When chemicals mix together and give off light it is called **chemiluminescence.**

ROLLER COASTERS

Although roller coasters throw you up and down hills at thrilling speeds, engineers have worked out how to make the ride go by itself, without the power of an engine. Actually, engines turn on just once in a rollercoaster ride – to pull the roller coaster up the first hill. After that, natural forces power the ride.

Once the roller coaster is past the top of the first hill, gravity takes over and pulls the ride down.

DRONING ON

A drone is a sort of robot that can do its job without a human being there with it. There are drones that work on land and sea but flying drones are becoming more and more popular because they are so useful. A flying robot with a camera attached to it can get to places and see things that humans cannot – and it can do it more quietly than a human in a helicopter!

When the roller coaster starts going down that first drop, it goes so fast it gathers enough energy to send it all the way up the next hill – and so on, as it whizzes around the whole ride. At the end of the ride, the roller coaster needs to put on the brakes to get rid of the energy and stop the ride.

43

COMPUTER ENGINEERING

Computer engineers design and build computers to help make our lives easier in a huge number of ways. Computers are part of our everyday lives – and not just the computers you write and play on. Household devices like washing machines and digital radios have computers inside them as well.

CODING

Coding is a way of giving instructions to a computer. It's a bit like talking to the computer in its own language. There are two main steps to coding. First, you need to think about the thing you want the computer to do. This could be something like getting dressed in the morning or finding the quickest route to a place. Then you need to break down that thing into a series of instructions. Most importantly, they need to be in the right order!

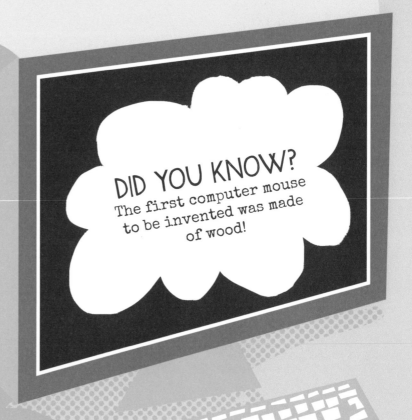

DID YOU KNOW?
The first computer mouse to be invented was made of wood!

WORLD WIDE WEB

The internet is the way computers are connected to each other all over the world. They might be linked by wires or without wires, called **wireless.** You can use the internet to send email messages, chat online and make phone or video calls. You can also search for information on the web or World Wide Web (www). Websites are pages of information linked together by the internet. You find those pages through a web browser.

QUIZ QUESTION:

When you visit a website, they often store small amounts of information on your computer to remember you on your next visit.
What is this information called?

a) crisps
b) cookies
c) biscuits

HOUSEHOLD ENGINEERING

Technology helps us with day-to-day tasks that we often don't even think about. But in many parts of the world we now think of this technology as essential to our lives, and we would struggle to get by without it!

SPIN CYCLE

Have you tried washing any clothes by hand? It's very hard work. In the past, women were expected to do most of the household laundry, so washing machines made a big difference to their daily lives. Washing machines automatically fill up with water, add soap powder or liquid, heat up the water, jumble the clothes around so the dirt falls off, rinse them several times and then spin them to dry them as much as possible!

UNDER PRESSURE

We use taps to turn the water on and off in our homes. The taps are attached to the hot and cold-water pipes. Inside each tap are two discs with holes in them. When you turn the tap, the discs slide across each other to open or close the holes. The water in the pipes is under pressure. This means it is pushing against the discs so when they line up the hole opens and the water gushes out.

TOILET TROUBLES

The modern toilet means we can flush away our wastewater (poo and wee) safely and keep our neighbourhoods clean and free from disease.

In the past, wastewater would be thrown into the streets and it was impossible to stop horrible smells and diseases. Now when you flush the toilet, water rushes into the bowl and clears out the wastewater. This runs along pipes out of the house, under the street and to a special sewage treatment centre. This treats the water until it's clean enough to go back into the rivers again!

ANSWERS

page 9
(b) spacecraft

page 7
(b) current

page 13
(a) the Sun

page 19
(b) the universe

page 25
(c) 1,000

page 15
(c) force

page 35
(a) less than 50 years ago

page 37
(c) both of the above

page 45
(b) cookies

page 40
(c) Japan